**A good name
keeps its lustre in the dark.**

Old English Proverb

The
ETIQUETTE
of
NAMING THE BABY

Copper Beech Publishing

Published in Great Britain by
Copper Beech Publishing Ltd
Copyright © Copper Beech Publishing Ltd 1996

ISBN 1 898617 14 7

A CIP catalogue record for this book is available from the
British Library.

Compiled from Victorian collections by Julie Lessels
Editor: Jan Barnes
Thanks to Guinness Publishing for permission to reproduce
the top twenty first names for girls and boys, England and
Wales, 1850 and 1900.
Taken from The Guinness Book of Names 7th Edition
Copyright © Leslie Dunkling & Guinness Publishing 1995.

Copper Beech Gift Books
Copper Beech Publishing Ltd
P O Box 159 East Grinstead
Sussex England RH19 4FS

Choosing a name is a very special gift you give to your child.

In this small volume, we are delighted to offer you a selection of traditional names used in Victorian times.

Name your baby after royalty, inventors, politicians, writers, explorers and other people with a place in history.

GIRLS
Top twenty first names for girls,
England and Wales★

	1850		1900
1	Mary	1	Florence
2	Elizabeth	2	Mary
3	Sarah	3	Alice
4	Ann	4	Annie
5	Eliza	5	Elsie
6	Jane	6	Edith
7	Emma	7	Elizabeth
8	Hannah	8	Doris
9	Ellen	9	Dorothy
10	Martha	10	Ethel
11	Emily	11	Gladys
12	Harriet	12	Lilian
13	Alice	13	Hilda
14	Margaret	14	Margaret
15	Maria	15	Winifred
16	Louisa	16	Lily
17	Fanny	17	Ellen
18	Caroline	18	Ada
19	Charlotte	19	Emily
20	Susannah	20	Violet

★Taken from *The Guinness Book of Names*.

Abigail *(Hebrew)* ~ 'A father's joy'.
Name your baby after Abigail, one of the wives of King David and a heroine of the scriptures.

Ada *(Anglo-Saxon)* ~ 'Rich gift' or 'happiness'.

Adelaide *(Teutonic)* ~ 'Noble maiden'.
Name your baby after Queen Adelaide (1792–1849) who was married to William IV.

Alethea *(Greek)* ~ 'Openness and sincerity'. A name used in England as far back as the 15th century.

Amelia *(Teutonic)* ~ 'Energetic' or 'hard worker'.

Alexandra *(Greek)* ~ 'Defender of men'.
Name your baby after Alexandra (1844–1925), who married the eldest son of Queen Victoria - the future Edward VII in 1863. She founded the Queen Alexandra's Royal Army Nursing Corps.

Alice and **Alicia** *(Old English)* ~ 'Noble'. A derivative of the Anglo-Saxon Ethel.
Name your baby after Princess Alice, daughter of Queen Victoria and Prince Albert.

Amy *(Latin)* ~ 'Beloved'.

Angelica *(Greek)* ~ 'A message from God'. **Angelique**, **Angela**, and **Angelina**, are variants.

Ann *(Hebrew)* ~ 'Grace, mercy, or favour'. The many different forms of this name show its extreme popularity. Among them, **Anne, Annie, Anna, Annette, Nancy and Hannah**.
Name your baby after Queen Anne who reigned 1702-1714; Anna Sewell (1820-78) who wrote the book 'Black Beauty' in 1877.

Annabella/Annabel *(Teutonic)* ~ 'Eagle heroine'. It is not a compound of Ann, since it is a much older name. Another form is **Arabella**.

Beatrice, Beatrix *(Latin)* ~ 'Joy-giver'.
Name your baby after Beatrix Potter, creator of 'Peter Rabbit', born 1866. The youngest daughter of Queen Victoria was named Beatrice.

Bertha *(Teutonic)* ~ 'Bright or shining one'.

Beryl *(Greek)* ~ A jewel name.

Blanche *(Teutonic)* ~ 'White'. A very ancient name, and extremely popular in former centuries.

Brenda *(Teutonic)* ~ 'A sword'.

Bridget *(Celtic)* ~ 'Strength'. Popular Irish name. **Bridgit**, **Brigid**, and **Biddy** are all variants.

Calypso *(Greek)* ~ 'Hider' or 'concealer'.

Camilla *(Latin)* ~ 'Attendant at a sacrifice'. A classical name adopted after the Reformation.

Carol *(Latin)* ~ 'To sing'.

Caroline *(Teutonic)* ~ 'Noble spirited'. This is the feminine form of the name Karl, which produces our English Charles, often used as a royal name.

Catherine *(Greek)* ~ 'Pure, unspotted'. **Catharina** and **Catharine** are variants of this name. Henry VIII had three wives by this name; Catherine of Aragon, Catherine Howard and Catherine Parr. There are various ways of spelling this name. In Old English, spelling was not considered important - even the person concerned might vary it!

Charity *(Greek)* ~ 'Kind-hearted'. One of the three sisters known as the charities or graces. An English variant is **Cherry**.

Charlotte *(Teutonic)* ~ 'Noble-minded'. A shortened version is **Lotty**.
Name your baby after Charlotte Bronte (1816-1855), the author of 'Jane Eyre'.

And the best and the worst of this is
That neither is most to blame
If you have forgotten my kisses
And I have forgotten your name.

Chloe *(Greek)* ~ 'Blooming'.

Christine *(Greek)* ~ 'A Christian' or 'A follower of Christ'. **Christiana, Christina, Chrissie, Christabel** are English variants of this name.
Name your baby after Christabel Pankhurst, suffragette and daughter of Emmeline.

11

Clara, Clare *(Latin)* ~ 'Famous'. From the masculine Clarus, a famous Roman name, Clara is the feminine form used in England, Germany and Spain. Other forms are **Clarice, Clarissa** and **Claire**.

Name your baby after Clare, a thirteenth-century saint, founder of the order of Franciscan nuns called the 'Poor Clares', whose main work involved the education and welfare of poor girls.

Claudia *(Latin)* ~ 'Lame'. In Wales Claudia became transformed into Gladys, whence it returned to England as a new name.

☆

Clementine *(Latin)* ~ 'Gentle'.

☆

Constance *(Latin)* ~ 'Firm'.

☆

Cynthia *(Greek)* ~ 'Moon-goddess'.

☆

Daphne *(Greek)* ~ 'A bay tree'.

Deborah *(Hebrew)* ~ 'A bee'.

Dora *(Greek)* ~ 'A gift'. Other forms are **Dorothy** and **Dorothea**, shortened to **Dolly**.

Dulce *(Latin)* ~ 'Sweet'.

Mutato nomine de te
Fabula narratur.
Change the name, and the tale is about you.
Horace 65-8BC

Elizabeth *(Hebrew)* ~ 'Oath of God'. With the exception of Mary, no other name has so many derivatives, variants and diminutives. **Babette, Bess, Bessie, Bet, Beth, Betsy, Bettina, Betty, Eliza, Elsbet, Elspeth, Elsa, Elsie, Lilibeth, Lilibet, Lisbeth, Lisa, Lise, Lil, Lily, Lilly, Lillie, Liz, Lizzy, Lizzie, Liza**.

Name your baby after Queen Elizabeth I (1533-1603); Elizabeth Fry (1778-1845), celebrated prison reformer; Elizabeth Gaskell (1810-1865), Victorian novelist; Elizabeth Barrett Browning (1806-1861), poet.

Edith *(Teutonic)* ~ 'Rich gift'.

Ellen *(Greek)* ~ 'Light'. Another form is **Eleanor**.

Emily *(Latin)* ~ 'Flattering' or *(Teutonic)* ~ 'Work'. Name your baby after Emily Bronte (1818-1848) who wrote 'Wuthering Heights'.

Emma *(Teutonic)* ~ An old German name from the word 'a nurse'.

Emmeline *(Teutonic)* ~ 'Work'. Name your baby after Emmeline Pankhurst, who founded the National Union of Women's Suffrage Societies in 1897.

Enid *(Celtic)* ~ 'The soul'. Name your baby after Enid, the wife of Prince Geraint, one of the Knights of the Round Table.

Ethel *(Teutonic)* ~ 'Noble'. In Anglo-Saxon times this name never stood alone, but was always linked to another, Ethel being really regarded as an adjective qualifying its connecting noun.

Eugenia, Eugenie *(Greek)* ~ 'Nobly born'.

Eve *(Hebrew)* ~ 'Life', since Eve was regarded as the mother of all living.

Faith *(Latin)* ~ this name belongs to the class of 'abstract virtue names' which includes such as Hope, Patience and Charity.

☆

Fanny *(Teutonic)* ~ 'Pretty'.

☆

Felicity *(Latin)* ~ 'Happiness'.

☆

Flora *(Latin)* ~ 'A flower'. Flora was the Roman goddess of spring and the flowers.

☆

Florence *(Latin)* ~ 'Flowering'. This name was used for both sexes in the Middle Ages!
Name your baby after 'the lady with the lamp' - Florence Nightingale (1820-1910).

☆

Frances *(Teutonic)* ~ 'Free-woman'.
Francesca ~ A beautiful Italian form of Frances.
Freda ~ A popular form, meaning 'peace'.

Gabrielle *(Hebrew)* ~ 'Heroine of God' or 'God is my strength'.

Gemma *(Latin)* ~ 'A jewel'.

Genevieve *(Celtic)* ~ 'White wave'.

Georgina *(Greek)* ~ Popular English contraction of Georgiana. **Georgy** and **Georgette** are diminutives of the same.

Geraldine *(Teutonic)* ~ 'Firm spear'.

Germaine *(Teutonic)* ~ 'Housewife'.

Gertrude *(Teutonic)* ~ 'Spear-maiden'. **Gatty** is an English contraction.

Gillian *(Latin)* ~ 'Downy or soft-haired'. This is the English variant of Julia.

Gloria *(Latin)* ~ 'Glowing or shining forth'.

Glorianna ~ An Elizabethan compound name - 'Glorious and peaceful'. Poetically used in reference to the Virgin Queen.

*She is born in a good hour
Who gets a good name.*

Grace *(Latin)* ~ 'Thanksgiving'. **Gracie** is an English diminutive of this name.

Gwendolen *(Celtic)* ~ 'White browed'. This very pretty name, has an extremely large number of derivatives and variants, all those commencing with 'Gwen' being purely Welsh.

Hannah *(Hebrew)* ~ 'Grace', early version of Anne.

Harriet *(Teutonic)* ~ 'Home-ruler'. This name is derived from Heimdal, the sword-god in Teutonic mythology, who acted as watchman at one end of the rainbow.

Hebe *(Greek)* ~ 'Youthful beauty'.

Helen *(Greek)* ~ 'Brightly shining one'. Helena is both the Spanish form and English variant.
Name your baby after the mythological Helen of Troy, whose beauty dazzled her countless admirers. When the Trojan prince, Paris, came as a guest of her husband's court he fell in love with Helen, and carried her back to Troy with him.

Henrietta *(Teutonic)* ~ 'Home ruler'. The English feminine form of Henry.
Name your baby after Henrietta Maria (1601-1669) who was the French wife of Charles I of England.

Hilary *(Latin)* ~ 'Cheerful'. Originally the masculine form of Hilaria, this has virtually dropped into disuse, and Hilary is now used for girls or boys.

A good name
is better than precious ointment ...
Ecclesiastes

Hilda *(Teutonic)* ~ 'Battle-maid'. One of the very oldest of Teutonic names, descended from the Valkyries, the warrior-maidens of Scandinavian mythology. The three commonest root-words of old Teutonic names were all indicative of courage, Hilda 'battle'; Gunda 'brave' and Trud 'fortitude'.

Hope ~ An abstract virtue name, forming the trio with Faith and Charity.

Ida *(Teutonic)* ~ 'Perfect happiness'.

Imogen ~ An Old English name found in Shakespeare's play 'Cymbeline'.

Irene *(Latin)* ~ 'Messenger of peace'.

Iris *(Greek)* ~ 'A messenger'. In classical mythology, Iris was the messenger of the gods.

Isabel *(Hebrew)* ~ 'God hath sworn', or 'God's oath'. A variant of Elizabeth, used both in England and Scotland. **Bella** is a shortened form; **Isabella** is a Spanish form.

Ivanna *(Hebrew)* ~ 'Grace of God'.

Ivy *(Teutonic)* ~ 'Clinging'. Ivy has been made the symbol of friendship and fidelity.

Jane *(Hebrew)* ~ 'Grace of the Lord'. This name comes from the same root as Hannah. **Janet, Jannette** are Scottish variations.

Name your baby after Jane Austen (1775-1817), famous English novelist.

Jasmine ~ A flower name, meaning amiability.

Jean *(Hebrew)* ~ 'Grace of the Lord'.

Jemima *(Hebrew)* ~ 'A dove'.

Jennifer *(Celtic)* ~ 'White wave'. The Cornish form of Guinevere. A shortened version is **Jenny**.

Jessica *(Hebrew)* ~ 'Grace of the Lord'. **Jessie** is the popular English contraction of Jessica.

Jocasta *(Greek)* ~ 'Twice-wedded'.

Joanna *(Hebrew)* ~ 'The Lord's grace'.

Joy ~ 'Gladness'. Joy stands alone as one of our abstract virtue names.

> *"I have no name*
> *I am but two days old. –"*
> *"What shall I call thee?"*
> *"I happy am*
> *Joy is my name, –"*
> *"Sweet joy befall thee!"*
> **Infant Joy –William Blake**

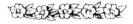

Julia, Julie *(Latin)* ~ 'Soft-haired'. Julia in early centuries was one of the most famous names among Roman women. It was used as an English name principally during the seventeenth and eighteenth centuries. **Juliette** is an Italian derivative.

Karin *(Teutonic)* ~ 'Pure'.

Katharine *(Greek)* ~ 'Pure' or 'unspotted'. Besides meaning purity, the name also implies beauty, grace and intellectual devotion. Apart from the saints and holy women who have borne the name, the pages of history can supply both famous and infamous bearers of it. Katharine of France, the adored wife of Henry V, the victor of Agincourt, and Catherine of Braganza. **Katherine** is the English variant. **Kate** and **Kitty** are other forms.

Kathleen *(Greek)* ~ 'Purity'. **Katty** is a diminutive.

Lara *(Latin)* ~ 'Talkative'.

Laura *(Latin)* ~ 'Laurel bay tree'.

Leah *(Hebrew)* ~ 'Weary'. This was the name of Laban's eldest daughter, who was given to Jacob for a wife.

Letitia *(Latin)* ~ 'Joy'. **Lettice** and **Letty** are variants of this. Letty being the common diminutive in England.

Name your baby after Lettice Knollys, lady-in-waiting to Elizabeth I.

Libby *(Hebrew)* ~ 'God hath sworn'. Contraction of Elizabeth.

Lilian *(Latin)* ~ 'Purity', of which a white lily is the emblem. **Lily** is a common diminutive.

Louisa *(Teutonic)* ~ 'Praise and fame'.
Name your baby after Louisa May Alcott (1832-88) the author of children's stories, one of which was 'Little Women'.

Lucinda *(Latin)* ~ 'Light'. **Lucy** is another form.

Lydia *(Greek)* ~ 'Melody'.

What's in a name? - that which we call a rose.
By any other name would smell as sweet.
Romeo and Juliet - William Shakespeare.

Mab *(Celtic)* ~ 'Mirth'. An Irish heroine bore the name Meadhbh, and her story became folk-lore. She was transformed into the Queen of the Fairies, under the name of Mab, whence the name was transferred to England in Elizabethan times.

Mabel *(Latin)* ~ 'Beloved' or 'beautiful one'.

Madeleine *(Hebrew)* ~ 'She came from Magdala'.

Margaret *(Greek)* ~ 'A pearl' - one of the dainty 'jewel' names. Popular diminutives are **Maisie**, **Madge** and **Meg**.

Marguerite ~ French variant often changed into the pet diminutive '**Daisy**'.

Marian, **Marion** ~ An English form of Mary, popularised in 'Maid Marian and Robin Hood'.

Martha, Marta (Hebrew) ~ 'Becoming bitter'. This name has become a synonym for an energetic, busy housewife, in reference to the Gospel Martha, the sister of Lazarus and Mary, of whom we read she 'was cumbered about much serving'.

I have a passion for the name of 'May'
For once it was a magic sound to me.
Don Juan - Byron

Mary *(Hebrew)* ~ 'Bitter'. English form of the name. **May** is a popular English contraction, other variants include; **Maria, Marie, Maureen, Marilyn, Marylyn, Mari, Marianne, Marianna, Molly.** Name your baby after Mary Ann Evans who wrote under the pseudonym of George Eliot in the 19th century. Perhaps her most famous works are 'Silas Marner' and 'Middlemarch'. Marie Curie (1867-1934), French physicist.

Mathilda *(Teutonic)* ~ 'Mighty battle-maid'. The English form is Matilda.

Melissa *(Latin)* ~ 'A bee'.

Mercy ~ 'Merciful'. A favourite Old English name, like Faith and Hope, this is an abstract virtue name, and was favoured by the Puritans. In diminutive form it is **Merry**.

Millicent *(Teutonic)* ~ 'Work, strength'.

Minerva *(Latin)* ~ 'Wisdom'. Name your baby after the Roman goddess who presided over the arts, poetry, spinning and weaving.

Miranda *(Latin)* ~ 'To be admired'.

Modesty ~ One of the Puritan abstract virtue names.

Myrtle *(English)* ~ 'Love'. A flower name.

Nan *(Hebrew)* ~ 'Grace'. English contraction of Hannah.

Nancy is the English variant, meaning 'joyful'.

Naomi *(Hebrew)* ~ 'Pleasant'.

Natasha *(Latin)* ~ 'Christmas child'.

Nellie *(Greek)* ~ 'Light'.

Octavia *(Latin)* ~ 'The eighth'. An Italian feminine form of Octavius.

Olivia *(Latin)* ~ 'The olive', symbol of peace. A form of Olive first used in Queen Anne's time.

Patience *(Latin)* ~ 'Bearing up'. Possessing quality of quiet endurance.

Prudence *(Latin)* ~ 'Prudent'. Well-loved by the Puritans.

Rachel *(Hebrew)* ~ 'Ewe'. The wife of Jacob in the Bible.

Rebecca *(Hebrew)* ~ 'To bind'.

Rosemary *(Latin)* ~ 'Dew of the sea' or *(Hebrew)* 'Mary's rose'.

Ruth *(Hebrew)* ~ 'Beauty'. An Old Testament name, favoured by the Puritans.

Sarah *(Hebrew)* ~ 'The princess'.

Shirley ~ Originally only used as a surname and boys' Christian name. First used as a fictional heroine's name by Charlotte Bronte.

Sophie *(Greek)* ~ 'Wisdom'.

Stephanie *(Greek)* ~ 'Crown of victory'.

Susan *(Hebrew)* ~ 'Lily'. **Susannah** is another form.

Tabitha *(Hebrew)* ~ 'A gazelle'.

Theresa *(Greek)* ~ 'The reaper'.

Thora *(Teutonic)* ~ 'Born of the thunder'.

Ursula *(Latin)* ~ 'Bear'.

Vera *(Slavonic)* ~ 'Grace of love and faith'.

Victoria *(Latin)* ~ 'Triumphal conqueror'.
Name your baby after Queen Victoria (1819-1901).

Violet *(Latin)* ~ 'Symbol of modesty'.

A name and also an omen.
Plautus

Winifred *(Celtic)* ~ 'White stream'.

Wilhelmina *(Teutonic)* ~ 'Helmet of resolution'.

BOYS

*Top twenty first names for boys,
England and Wales* ★

	1850		1900
1	William	1	William
2	John	2	John
3	George	3	George
4	Thomas	4	Thomas
5	James	5	Charles
6	Henry	6	Frederick
7	Charles	7	Arthur
8	Joseph	8	James
9	Robert	9	Albert
10	Samuel	10	Ernest
11	Edward	11	Robert
12	Frederick	12	Henry
13	Alfred	13	Alfred
14	Richard	14	Sidney
15	Walter	15	Joseph
16	Arthur	16	Harold
17	Benjamin	17	Harry
18	David	18	Frank
19	Edwin	19	Walter
20	Albert	20	Herbert

★Taken from *The Guinness Book of Names*.

Aaron *(Hebrew)* ~ 'High mountain'.

☆

Abraham *(Hebrew)* ~ 'Father of a multitude'.

☆

Adam ~ 'The red earth'.

☆

Albert *(Teutonic)* ~ 'Noble splendour'.
Name your baby after Prince Albert who married
Queen Victoria in February 1840.

☆

Alexander *(Greek)* ~ 'Helper of men'.
Name your baby after Macedonian king, Alexander
the Great (356–322 BC).
Alastair is a form of Alexander.

☆

Alfred *(Teutonic)* ~ 'Elf fairy'.

☆

Allen *(Celtic)* ~ 'Ploughed up grass land'.

☆

Ambrose *(Greek)* ~ 'Immortal' or 'joyful hope' of everlasting life.

Amos *(Hebrew)* ~ 'Bearer of burdens', 'strong'.

Giving a name, indeed, is a poetic art.
Carlyle 1832

Andrew *(Greek)* ~ 'A king' or 'a man'.

Antony *(Latin)* ~ 'Much esteemed'.

Arthur *(Celtic)* ~ 'High' or 'noble'. This name was made famous by King Arthur and his knights of the round table.
Name your baby after Prince Arthur (1486-1502), the eldest son of Henry VII.

Ashley *(Old English)* ~ 'Builder'. Ash tree in a meadow.

Bartholomew *(Hebrew)* ~ 'Son of the furrows'.

Barnabas, Barnaby *(Hebrew)* ~ 'Son of consolation'.

Benjamin *(Hebrew)* ~ 'Son of my right hand'. Name your baby after British Prime Minister and novelist, Benjamin Disraeli (1804–1881).

Bernard *(Teutonic)* 'Firm bear'.

Bertram *(Teutonic)* ~ 'Bright raven'.

Caleb *(Hebrew)* ~ A name meaning 'a dog' (someone who is faithful). An Old Testament name, popular in England after the Reformation.

Callum *(Celtic)* ~ 'Dove'.

I shall give them an everlasting name,
that shall not be cut off.

Charles *(Teutonic)* ~ 'Man'.
Name your baby after two kings of Great Britain; Charles I (1600-49) and Charles II (1630-85); Charles Dickens (1812-1870), writer; Charles Darwin (1809-1882), the naturalist and scientist, who wrote 'Origin of Species' in 1859; Charles L. Dodgson who, under the pen name Lewis Carroll, wrote 'Alice's Adventures in Wonderland', published 1865.

Christopher *(Greek)* ~ 'Christ bearer'. St. Christopher, martyr, and deeply venerated, became the patron saint of protection against sickness, earthquake, fire and flood.

Name your baby after Sir Christopher Wren (1632-1723) who designed St. Paul's Cathedral.

Conrad *(Teutonic)* ~ 'Bold of speech'.

Crispin *(Latin)* ~ 'Curly hair'.

Daniel *(Hebrew)* ~ 'A judge'.

Darcy *(Celtic)* ~ 'Dark-haired'.

Darius *(Ancient Persian)* ~ 'King'.

David *(Hebrew)* ~ 'Beloved'.

Name your baby after St. David, patron saint of Wales. Welshmen still wear leeks in their hats on his feast day, 1st March.

Dominic *(Latin)* ~ 'Sunday child'.

Donald *(Celtic)* ~ 'Proud chief'.

Duncan *(Celtic)* - 'Brown chief'.

Edward *(Teutonic)* ~ 'The rich guardian'.
Name your baby after the three English Saxon kings
– Edward the Elder, Edward the Martyr and Edward
the Confessor.

Edwin *(Teutonic)* 'Rich friend'.

☆

Emanuel *(Hebrew)* ~ 'God with us'.

☆

Eugene *(Greek)* ~ 'Well-born'.

☆

Fergus *(Celtic)* ~ 'Man of strength'.

☆

Francis *(Teutonic)* ~ 'Free.' Frank is the English
form.
Name your baby after Sir Francis Drake (c.1540-96),
the great Elizabethan seaman.

☆

Frederick *(Teutonic)* ~ 'Peace ruler'. Also, **Fred**
and **Freddie**.

Gabriel *(Hebrew)* ~ 'Hero of God'. The archangel strengthened Daniel and brought the promise to Zacharias and to the Virgin Mary.

Galahad *(Old English)* ~ 'Milky way'.

Gawain *(Celtic)* ~ 'Plenty' or 'hawk of battle'. One of the best known of King Arthur's legendary round table knights was called Sir Gawain, who undertook to wed the 'loathly lady' and was rewarded by breaking the spell and discovering her loveliness.

Geoffrey *(Teutonic)* ~ 'Divine peace'.
Name your baby after Geoffrey Chaucer (c.1345-1400), English poet, famous for 'The Canterbury Tales'.

George *(Greek)* ~ 'Husbandman'. Georgios was the name of a Cappadocian saint and martyr to whose honour Constantine erected a church at Byzantium. He was the origin of the allegory of the warrior saint George contending with the dragon and delivering the oppressed Church. The Crusaders fixed on St. George as the miraculous champion whom they beheld fighting in their cause.

Name your baby after King George I, reigned 1714-1727, George II, 1727-1760, George III, 1760-1820, George IV, 1820-1830.

Gregory *(Greek)* ~ 'Watchman'.

Harold *(Teutonic)* ~ 'Warrior power'.
Name your baby after Harold 'Harefoot' ruled 1035-1040 and Harold II, fought William the Conqueror at the Battle of Hastings in 1066.

Henry *(Teutonic)* ~ 'Ruler of the home'.
Name your baby after the eight kings of England; Henry I - 1100-1135; Henry VIII who was famous for his many wives, ruled 1509-1547. **Harry** is the English form.

Horace, **Horatio** *(Latin)* ~ A Roman name.
Name your baby after Horatio Nelson, hero of the Battle of Trafalgar.

Hugh *(Teutonic)* ~ 'Mind'. **Hugo** is another English form.

Humphrey *(Teutonic)* ~ 'Support of peace'.

Ian *(Hebrew)* ~ 'Grace of the Lord'.

Isaac *(Hebrew)* ~ 'Laughter'.
Name your baby after Sir Isaac Newton (1642-1727), mathematician.

Ivor *(Teutonic)* ~ 'The archer'.

Jack *(Hebrew)* ~ 'Jehovah is gracious'.

Jacob *(Hebrew)* ~ 'Supplanter'. Biblical son of Isaac and Rebecca.

James *(Hebrew)* ~ 'Supplanter'.
Name your baby after James VI of Scotland, who became James I of England, uniting the two kingdoms in 1603.

Joel *(Hebrew)* ~ 'Strong-willed'.

John *(Hebrew)* ~ 'The Lord's Grace'. King John, who ruled 1199-1216 is often regarded as 'the worst of English kings'!

Jonathan *(Hebrew)* ~ 'Gift of God'.
Name your baby after Jonathan Swift (1667-1745), who wrote 'Gulliver's Travels'.

Jordan *(Hebrew)* ~ 'To descend'. The name is from the River Jordan.

Joseph *(Hebrew)* ~ An addition. A Scriptural name. After waiting long for a son, Rachel called hers Joseph because she hoped another would be added to her family.

Joshua *(Hebrew)* ~ 'Eternal salvation'.

Julian *(Latin)* ~ 'Downy bearded'.

Justin *(Latin)* ~ 'Just'.

Let us speak plain,
there is more force in names
than most men dream of.
J R Lowell

Karl *(Teutonic)* ~ 'God of the winds'.
Name your baby after Karl Marx (1818-1883), revolutionary thinker.

Kerry *(Anglo-Saxon)* ~ 'Captain'.

☆

Kevin *(Celtic)* ~ 'Kind' or 'fair'.

☆

Kieran *(Celtic)* ~ 'Black'.

☆

Laurence *(Latin)* ~ 'Laurel'. A shortened form is **Larry**.

Leonard *(Teutonic)* ~ 'Lion or strong'. Shortened forms are **Leo** and **Leon**.

Llewelyn *(Celtic)* ~ 'Lightning'.

Louis *(Teutonic)* ~'Famous war'. Three monarchs of the Karling line bore the name which became so essentially connected with French royalty that after the succession of the Bourbons, no member of the French royal family was christened without it.

Luke *(Latin)* ~ 'Light'.

Marcus *(Latin)* ~ 'Manly qualities'.

Mark *(Greek)* ~ 'Soft and tender'.

Matthew *(Hebrew)* ~ 'Gift of the Lord'.

Michael *(Hebrew)* ~ 'Who is like unto God'.
Name your baby after Michael Faraday (1791-1867), whose greatest achievement was the discovery of magneto-electricity.

Nathaniel *(Hebrew)* ~ 'Gift of God'.

Neill, **Neil** *(Celtic)* ~ 'Champion'.

Nicholas *(Greek)* ~ 'Victory of the people'. From Nikolaos. Nikolaos was the name of a Saint whom legend relates supplied three destitute maidens with marriage portions by secretly leaving money at their window. As his day occurred just before Christmas, he was thus made the supplier of the gifts of the season to all children in Flanders and Holland, who put out their shoe or stocking in the confidence that 'Santa Klaus of Kneeht Clobes' as they call him, will put in a present for good conduct before morning.

Noah *(Hebrew)* ~ 'Rest'.

Oliver *(Latin)* ~ 'Crowned with olives'.
Name your baby after Oliver Cromwell who ruled
1653-1658.

Oscar *(Teutonic)* ~ 'Divine spear'.
Name your baby after Oscar Wilde who wrote 'The
Importance of being Earnest' in 1895.

Owen *(Celtic)* ~ 'Young warrior'.

*My name may have buoyancy enough
to float upon the sea of time.*
William Gladstone 1827

Patrick *(Latin)* ~ 'Noble'.

Paul *(Latin)* ~ 'Little'.

Peter *(Greek)* ~ 'Stone'. **Piers** is another form. Name your baby after St. Peter, the patron saint of fishermen.

Philip *(Greek)* ~ 'Lover of horses'.

Quentin *(Latin)* ~ 'Fifth'.

Richard *(Teutonic)* ~ 'Stern king'.
Name your baby after Richard I ('Richard the Lionheart'), who reigned 1189-1199; Richard II 1377-1399; Richard III, 1483-1485.

Robert *(Teutonic)* ~ 'Bright fame'. This name came to England at the time of the Norman Conquest.
Name your baby after Robert Burns, 18th century poet. In 1829, Sir Robert Peel established a police force in London.

Robin *(Teutonic)* ~ 'Bright fame'.
Name your baby after Robin Hood, legendary outlaw, first chronicled in the 15th century.

Roland/Rowland *(Teutonic)* ~ 'Fame of the land'.

Name your baby after Sir Rowland Hill (1795-1879), who introduced the penny post in 1840.

Rupert *(Teutonic)* ~ An English form of Robert. Name your baby after Rupert Brooke, poet.

Yet shall thy name, conspicuous and sublime
Stand in the spacious fermament of time.
William Wordsworth

Samuel *(Hebrew)* ~ 'Asked of God'. From schama (to hear).
Name your baby after Samuel Pepys (1633-1703), famous diarist.

☆

Sebastian *(Greek)* ~ 'Venerable'.

☆

Seth *(Hebrew)* ~ 'Appointed'.

☆

Simon *(Greek)* ~ 'Obedient'.

☆

Steven *(Greek)* ~ 'Crown of victory'.

☆

Thomas *(Hebrew)* ~ 'Twin'.

Name your baby after Thomas Gainsborough, 18th century artist; Thomas Hardy, novelist and poet.

Timothy *(Latin)* ~ 'To honour and fear God'.

Toby *(Hebrew)* ~ 'A poet'.

Todd *(Teutonic)* ~ 'Ruler of the people'.

Tristram *(Celtic)* ~ 'Herald'.

Name your baby after Tristram Shandy, fictional hero of a novel by Laurence Sterne (1713–1768).

Theodore *(Greek)* ~ 'Divine gift'.

Valentine *(Latin)* ~ 'Healthy'.

Victor *(Latin)* ~ 'Triumphal conqueror'. Victor is a man of triumph, and the name was borne by various martyrs.

Vincent *(Latin)* ~ 'Conquering'.
Name your baby after the artist Vincent Van Gogh.

Walter (Teutonic) ~ 'Powerful warrior'.
Name your baby after Sir Walter Raleigh - explorer.

William *(Teutonic)* ~. 'Helmed by will'. A name
from Teutonic mythology.
Name your baby after William the Conqueror
(1066-1087); William Shakespeare (1564-1616);
William Blake, who engraved and published his
'Songs of Innocence' in 1789.

Zachary *(Hebrew)* ~ 'Remembrance of the Lord'.

The Etiquette Collection is a series of pocket-sized books full of social secrets and hints for correct conduct. Collect the set!

THE ETIQUETTE OF AN ENGLISH TEA

How to serve a perfect English afternoon tea; tea traditions, superstitions, recipes - including how to read your fortune in the tea-leaves afterwards.

THE ETIQUETTE OF AN ENGLISH PUDDING

Are you missing a good old-fashioned pudding?
English puddings - the traditional way.
Delicious recipes which have been used for over 100 years.

ETIQUETTE FOR GENTLEMEN

No real gentleman should be without these rules for correct conduct. The perfect gift for the gentleman in every woman's life!

For your free catalogue containing these and other Copper Beech Gift Books, write to:

Copper Beech Publishing Ltd
P O Box 159 East Grinstead Sussex England RH19 4FS

*Copper Beech specialises in gift books
inspired by the charm of the past.*

THE ETIQUETTE OF DRESS
Peep through the wardrobe of times gone by and discover
how to be properly dressed for all occasions.
A must for those who have ever asked
'What shall I wear?'

ETIQUETTE FOR COFFEE LOVERS
Coffee lovers will enjoy this look at the history of coffee
drinking, its secrets, recipes, hints and coffee chat. The
perfect companion for coffee time.

THE ETIQUETTE OF POLITENESS
Good sense and good manners.
How to be polite and well-bred at all times.

THE ETIQUETTE OF LOVE AND COURTSHIP
A guide for romantics.
Flirting, temptation, first impressions: essential
advice for lovers.

*Copper Beech Gift Books
are designed and printed
in Great Britain.*